THE
LAWRENCE WELK
SHOW

Then & Now

This book is dedicated to all of the talented performers who are, or have been, part of the Welk Musical Family—then and now. Special thanks also go to our friends at the Oklahoma Educational Television Authority and Public Broadcast Service (PBS) who continue to bring the Welk television show into millions of North American homes each week, thereby maintaining this unforgettable legacy.

The greatest gratitude is, however, saved for Fern Welk, Lawrence's wife of 60 years. She has been the quiet force supporting the man and his music. She has truly "kept a song in her heart."

**Lawrence & Fern on their 50th
Wedding Anniversary**

TABLE OF CONTENTS

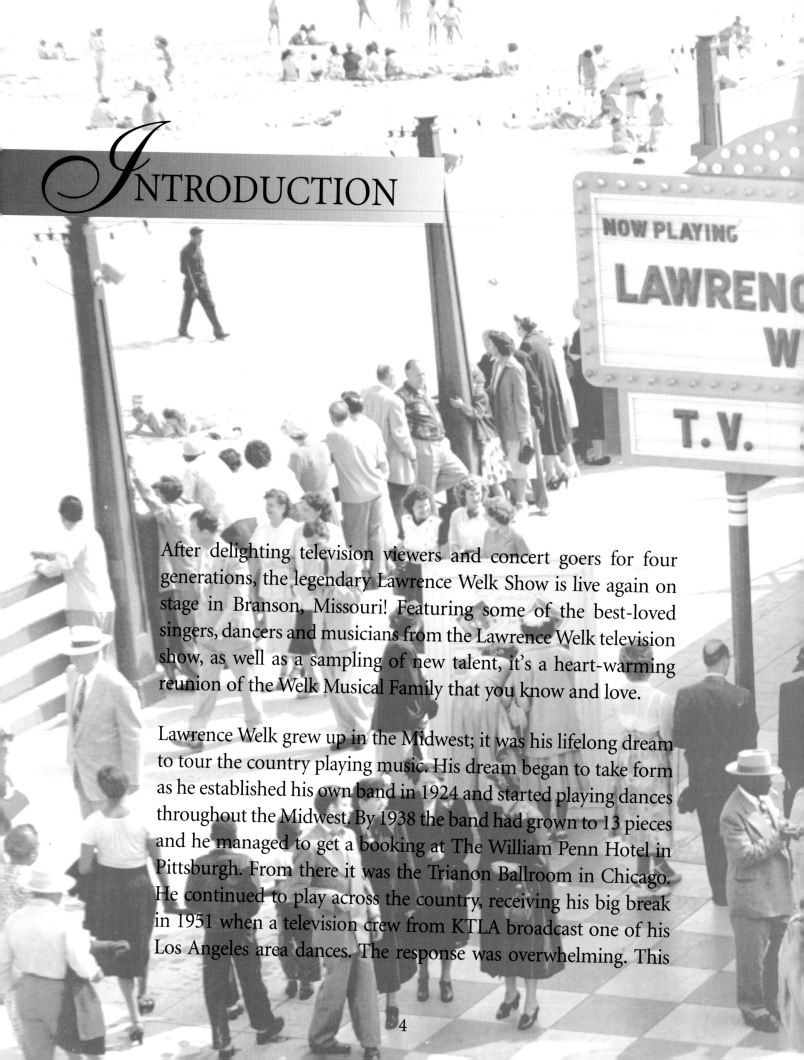

$\mathcal{I}$NTRODUCTION

After delighting television viewers and concert goers for four generations, the legendary Lawrence Welk Show is live again on stage in Branson, Missouri! Featuring some of the best-loved singers, dancers and musicians from the Lawrence Welk television show, as well as a sampling of new talent, it's a heart-warming reunion of the Welk Musical Family that you know and love.

Lawrence Welk grew up in the Midwest; it was his lifelong dream to tour the country playing music. His dream began to take form as he established his own band in 1924 and started playing dances throughout the Midwest. By 1938 the band had grown to 13 pieces and he managed to get a booking at The William Penn Hotel in Pittsburgh. From there it was the Trianon Ballroom in Chicago. He continued to play across the country, receiving his big break in 1951 when a television crew from KTLA broadcast one of his Los Angeles area dances. The response was overwhelming. This

marked the beginning of his renowned national prominence, with a four-year stint on KTLA in Los Angeles, 16 years on the ABC network and 11 years in syndication. The Lawrence Welk Show became the longest-running musical variety show in television history and continues today on Public Television.

Now, with the opening of the Welk Resort Center & Champagne Theatre in Branson, his dream has come full circle. Members of the musical family have returned home to the Midwest, continuing this American legacy.

CHILDHOOD YEARS

Born to German-Russian immigrants, in a sod farmhouse in North Dakota, Lawrence Welk was always drawn to music. In his autobiography "Wunnerful, Wunnerful" he wrote, "my earliest clear memory is crawling toward my father who was holding his accordion. I can still recall the wonder and delight I felt when he let me press my fingers on the keys and squeeze out a few wavering notes."

By the time he turned 17, Lawrence knew he could never be a farmer and that he really wanted to make music his life's work. In exchange for a $400 accordion, to be purchased by his dad, he agreed to stay on the farm and work for four more years.

On his 21st birthday, March 11, 1924, he left home to pursue his dream. He had little money and couldn't speak English, but what he did have was his accordion, his talent, and an overwhelming desire to succeed. His legendary life's work had just begun.

*Lawrence's mother –
Christina Schwahn Welk*

*Lawrence's father–
Ludwig Welk*

*This picture of Lawrence was taken soon
after he left the farm on his twenty-first
birthday, with an accordion, a change of
clothing, a few dollars, a Bible—and lots
of enthusiasm!*

EARLY BANDS

From the earliest days on the road, Lawrence never stopped trying to improve his band, and please his audience. His first bands included Welk's Novelty Orchestra, The Hotsy Totsy Boys and the Honolulu Fruit Gum Orchestra. These bands played throughout the Midwest, always looking for unique ways to delight the audience.

*Welk's
Novelty
Orchestra,
1920's*

*Eddie Ott's
Broadmoor Country
Club, Denver,
Colorado, 1931*

*Honolulu
Fruit Gum
Orchestra,
1920's*

WNAX Yankton S.D., 1928

9

ON THE ROAD

From The Roosevelt Hotel in New York to the Aragon Ballroom in Los Angeles, the Lawrence Welk Orchestra quickly became one of the famous "Big Bands" of the day, delighting audiences across the country with their "light, bubbly" sound, stylish dance routines and glamorous leading ladies. As members of the musical family will attest, Welk was a man who truly loved his audience, and went out of his way to charm and entertain them. His exuberance was infectious—effortlessly passed on to both band members and fans who reveled in his unique style of music-making.

Aragon Ballroom: Conga line at Lick Pier, Santa Monica, CA 1955

William Penn Hotel, Pittsburgh, PA, where Champagne Music was named in 1938

Trianon Ballroom in Chicago where Welk played for almost 10 years in the '40s

Elitch's Garden, 1947

Champagne Lady Helen Ramsey at the Roosevelt Hotel

Circa 1939

CHAMPAGNE LADIES

Norma Zimmer

The charming and talented "Champagne Ladies" each offered vocal stylings that defined the sound of Champagne Music. They were the signature piece for the Welk Orchestra. Through the years they waltzed in and out of the show, each leaving their own indelible mark. Lois Best was the first official Champagne Lady (1938-1940). She was followed by Jayne Walton (1940-1945), Joan Mowery (1945-1947), Helen Ramsey (1947-1949) and Roberta Linn (1949-1953). Alice Lon (1953-1959) was the first nationwide *television* Champagne Lady, known for her beautiful smile and frilly petticoats. Norma Zimmer was the last Champagne Lady appearing on the Welk Show from 1960 to 1982.

Roberta Linn

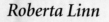

Joan Mowery

12

The Champagne Ladies loved to sing, and take a twirl around the dance floor with maestro Welk.

Helen
Ramsey

Lois Best

Jayne Walton

Alice Lon

13

ℐELEVISION

Lawrence was intent on producing a television show that would be welcome in everyone's home. From 1951-55, a local Los Angeles station, KTLA, televised the show. It was later picked up by the ABC network for a 16-year run, and then spent 11 years in syndication. During this time, Welk became known for his high-quality, family-oriented programming and to this day, his shows are still warming the hearts of America on Public Television.

The band in an early photo from a 1965 television show

The Aragon Ballroom as seen on KTLA–Champagne Lady Alice Lon dancing with Dick Dale

The annual
Christmas show and introduction of
performers' families, circa late '50s

Dodge was a sponsor
of the Lawrence
Welk Show, both
nationally and
locally. The show's
first producer, Ed
Sobol, is at the
left; next to him is
Director/
Producer,
Jim Hobson

MEMORABLE SHOWS

Special theme shows were the highlight of every Saturday night. Each program offered fans exciting costumes and stage sets, as well as spotlighting the many talents of the cast who performed a wide range of song and dance routines. The Patriotic Show (above) was a "spine-tingling" tribute to Lawrence's deep belief in the great American Dream and the principles of Democracy that founded this country.

Champagne Lady, Norma Zimmer singing "God Bless America"

16

At the close of each Christmas show, Santa arrived with presents for the children

The Lawrence Welk Christmas Show was the highest rated broadcast of the season. Lawrence and members of his cast introduced their families, often showcasing the budding talents of their children.

Dick Dale played Santa Claus.

From Christmas and New Years to Halloween and St. Patrick's Day, every holiday was cause for celebration! Musical family members brought a bit of holiday magic into the lives of their viewers.

The Easter Chorus

Anacani and Larry Hooper prepare for St. Patrick's Day

Ralna English and Kathie Sullivan celebrate the New Year with Lawrence

Thanksgiving

Bob Lido, Tanya and Charlie Parlato on the "Italian" special

Gail, Sandi and Mary Lou performing "Glow Little Glow Worm"

One of the most popular acts on the Welk show during the television years was Guy Hovis and Ralna English. Here they sing a country tune.

Just about everyone loved to sing and dance. Above: A Dutch "vacation" show. Right: A dance number from "Singin' In The Rain."

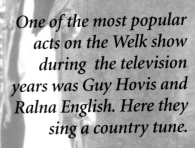

TV Musical Family

Tanya Falan

Kathie Sullivan

The success of the show was the strong bond felt between the "viewing family" and the "musical family" each Saturday night. Lawrence's desire to always please his fans won him loyalty, warmth and respect.

Here's a look back at some of the Champagne Music Makers that sang and danced their way into your hearts.

Aldridge Sisters &
Otwell Twins

Jim Turner

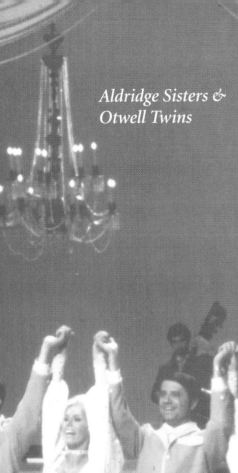

Bobby Burgess &
Cissy King

Sandi & Sally

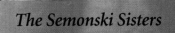

The Semonski Sisters

The Welk Entertainers were the best of the best. Beyond talent, Lawrence also looked for that special blend, sound or feature which now has characterized this American televison legacy.

Natalie Nevins
and Irish tenor Joe Feeney

Bob Ralston played
organ and piano

Larry Hooper and Mary Lou Metzger

Clay Hart and Salli Flynn who later became husband and wife

Jack Imel, always the clown, and Mary Lou Metzger

Barbara Boylan and Bobby Burgess

23

THE LAWRENCE WELK ORCHESTRA

The effervescent sounds of the Lawrence Welk Orchestra typified what America wanted to hear, from polkas to popular classics, the band always maintained a light, bright, happy style—perfect for dancing!

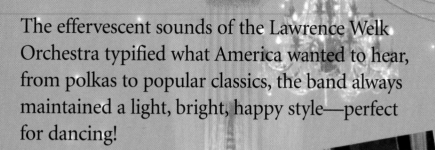

The brass section blowing their horns!

The string section with Bob Ralston

Charlotte Harris and Frank Scott with the string section, 1960's

The Hotsy Totsy Boys perform Dixieland—Lawrence's favorite

Johnny Klein (left), Lawrence's
cousin, and Jack Imel (right) on
the drums

Buddy Merrill and Neil Le Vang
with Lawrence in the center

Right: Musical Director George Cates is a genius when
it comes to music. Like his boss, he is completely devoted
to the audience. Above: The wonderful reed section

LAWRENCE

What was it that endeared him to the public? Part of it was his music and his dedication to his audience. Another part was his innate charm and unassuming "niceness." His warm heart embraced every fan and every performer. People responded to the love that flowed from him so freely.

Above left: Lawrence Welk had great fun on stage!
Above: The cast surprised him with a 70th birthday cake on the show. Right: He dressed up as a hippie in 1969; stagehands at Harrah's/Tahoe, where he was playing, didn't recognize him and wouldn't let him on stage until he was able to prove his true identity.

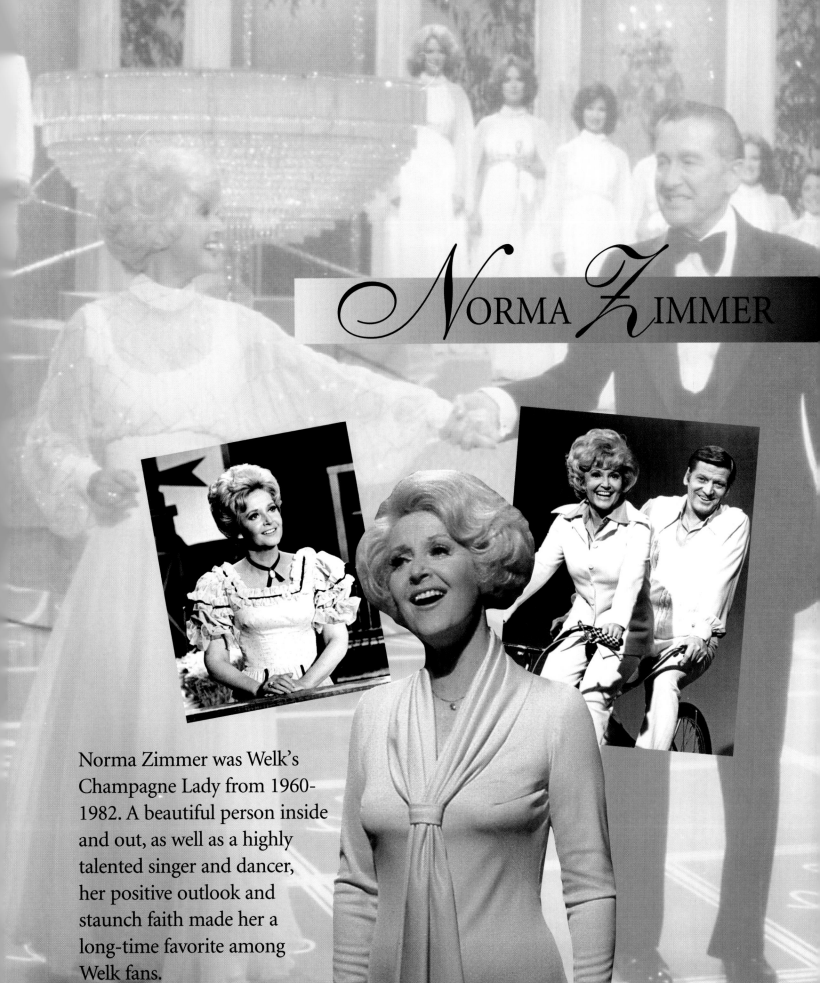

Norma Zimmer

Norma Zimmer was Welk's Champagne Lady from 1960-1982. A beautiful person inside and out, as well as a highly talented singer and dancer, her positive outlook and staunch faith made her a long-time favorite among Welk fans.

Lawrence Welk & The Champagne Music Makers, 1980's

WELK RESORT CENTER &
CHAMPAGNE THEATRE

The hills of Branson are alive with the sounds
of Champagne Music.

Designed for music lovers and Welk fans of all ages,
the Welk Resort Center & Champagne Theatre offers
unbeatable musical entertainment from morning
'til night. Days begin with the classic harmonies of
the Lennon Brothers Breakfast Show featuring the
best-loved hits of the '30s, '40s and '50s performed
by the Lennon Sisters' talented brothers, sister-in-law
Gail and Peggy's son Mike. During the day, hotel
guests can mingle with Welk "stars" and enjoy resort
amenities and shopping. Live musical performances
of the Lawrence Welk Show are presented in the
Champagne Theatre.

For a bite to eat before or after the show, the Stage
Door Canteen Restaurant is the perfect setting for
those who enjoy fine food, music and fun.

The Champagne Theatre

The 160-room Welk Resort Hotel was designed to make everyone feel right at home. It includes pool, spa and sports activities and is located next to the Champagne Theatre and Stage Door Canteen Restaurant.

31

BRANSON MUSICAL FAMILY

The new Lawrence Welk Orchestra carries on the Champagne Music tradition under the direction of Larry Cansler

Musical Director, Larry Cansler

Andre Tayir, the producer/director, is the creative force behind the new Lawrence Welk Show

The performers in Branson dazzle the audience; whether it's a "Hollywood" theme or a country "Jambalaya" party, they are sure to keep toes tapping to the beat

Getting "In The Mood"

Lori Gier brings the crowds to their feet with her beautiful soprano voice

Michael and Lori Gier

Giving honor to our great nation

33

OZARK MOUNTAIN CHRISTMAS

The town of Branson is transformed into a Christmas wonderland. At Welk's Champagne Theatre, the beauty of Christmas is gloriously revealed in the form of an illuminated angel as the Lennon Sisters and Tom Netherton reverently sing "Silent Night." The spectacular Christmas Show incorporates heartwarming classics, and fun-filled caroling. There is nothing quite like a Welk Family Christmas. You are bound to feel like you're "home for the holidays."

The Christmas spirit is alive with trumpets blowing! Gail and Ron go caroling, while Mary Lou and Jack are "Walking in a Winter Wonderland." The Nutcracker Suite soldiers decorate the stage in lights.

Lori Gier

Jo Ann Castle

THE LENNON SISTERS

America fell in love with them as the girls next door, today they are an institution. Glamorous yet unpretentious, sophisticated yet down-to-earth, talented yet unassuming—it's no wonder they are adored.

Getting a star on the Hollywood Walk of Fame was a thrill for these "leading ladies"

The Lennon Sisters guest starred at the Ice Follies

They were just 9, 12, 14 and 16 when they joined the Lawrence Welk Show on Christmas Eve, 1955. For 13 years "The Girls" grew up on the show, transforming themselves from "America's Sweethearts" to "Sophisticated Ladies."

The Lennon Sisters arrive in Hawaii in 1959 for an on location shoot of the Lawrence Welk Show. They were already known as America's "Sweethearts of Song."

An Early American stage set at the ABC Studio; circa 1959

Donning Elizabethan gowns, "The Girls" performed a touching rendition of "Greensleeves"

The Lennon Sisters love Branson! Dee Dee, Peggy, Kathy and Janet pose after a show with Janet's husband John Bahler who is the Lennon's musical conductor and arranger.

This four-some is awesome. Well-known for their sweet-voiced harmonies, the Lennons are extremely talented individuals.

Larry Welk (center) joins "the girls" back stage just before the opening of the first Branson Show. Janet, Kathy, Peggy and DeeDee.

THE LENNON FAMILY

From left: Dianne's daughter, Dee Dee Gass; Peggy's daughters, Betsy & Jenny Cathcart; Janet's daughter, Kristin Bernhardi.

It's a Lennon Family reunion on stage in Branson!

The Lennon Sisters are joined by their brothers, sons and daughters

Making great music is a family
tradition. The Lennon Brothers,
Bill, Joe and Dan provide the
close harmony that gives this group
their distinctive swinging sound.
They are joined by their nephew,
Mike Cathcart who
plays piano and guitar
and Gail,
Bill's wife,
whose lead
vocals and
musical arrangements
create the classic
sounds of the 30's
40's and 50's.

Performing at the Stage Door Canteen

JO ANN CASTLE

She's the dynamic blonde piano player with an infectious personality and contagious smile. Known as the queen of ragtime piano, her exuberant performances have won her a loyal, loving following.

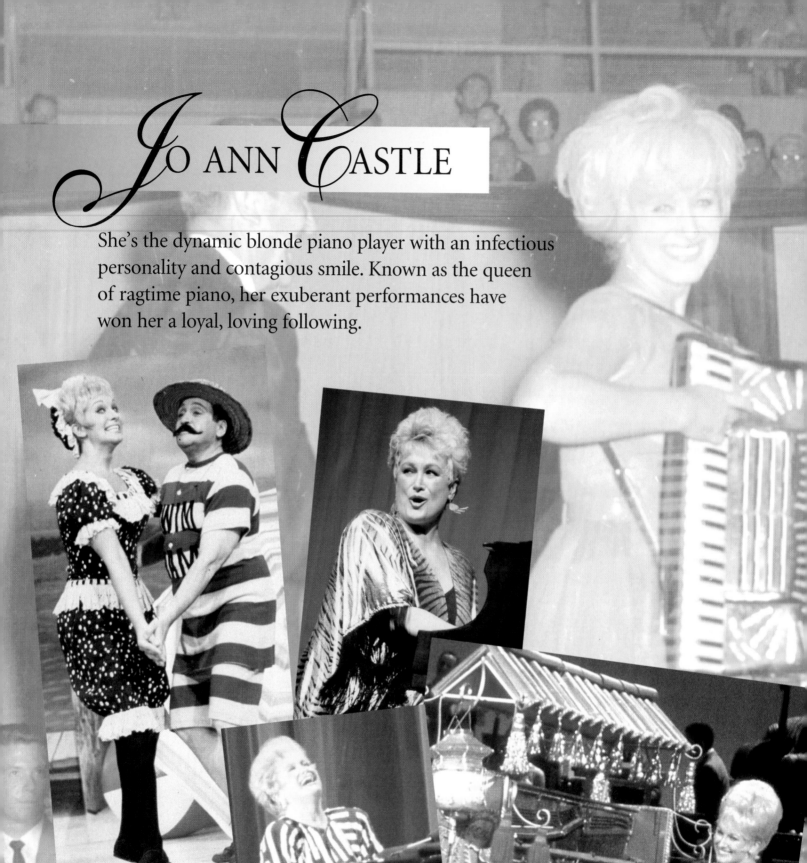

Jo Ann and Aladdin

Brewing up some goulish ragtime

Jo Ann earned a national reputation by performing (and clowning around on) the Lawrence Welk Television Show. Beyond ragtime she can, however, play all styles of music and is recognized for her tremendous versatility.

With Lawrence

MYRON FLOREN

He starred on the Lawrence Welk Television Show for 32 years and is widely recognized as one of the greatest accordionists in the world.

Myron loves to entertain. "It keeps me young," he says.

A dynamic singer and performer, "charismatic" is the word most frequently used to describe Ralna. She has been honored by the Gospel Music Association for her spirituals, which are now an unforgettable part of the Branson show.

Ralna manages to "touch" just about every member of the audience with her powerful voice.

45

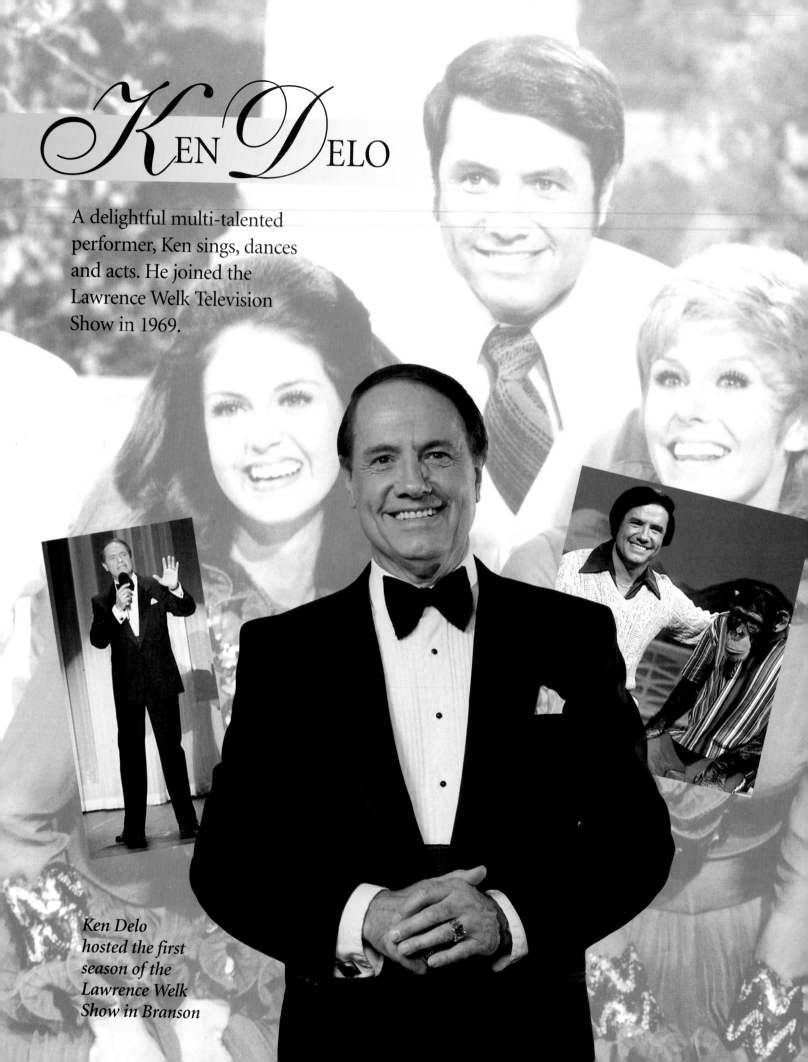

KEN DELO

A delightful multi-talented performer, Ken sings, dances and acts. He joined the Lawrence Welk Television Show in 1969.

Ken Delo hosted the first season of the Lawrence Welk Show in Branson

Pretty and effervescent, Mary Lou joined the Welk Musical Family in 1970 and has been a favorite with Welk television fans—and Branson fans—ever since.

MARY LOU METZGER

Gail and Mary Lou splashing around as mermaids

Mary Lou joins Jack Imel for rousing dance numbers

BOBBY BURGESS & ELAINE BALDEN

Audiences can't help being swept up in their fun! A perfect complement to one another, Bobby and Elaine first performed together on the Lawrence Welk T.V. Show in 1979 and have been performing together ever since.

Going "all out" on stage in Branson

Having worked together for over 15 years, they have developed an uncanny ability to synchronize their movements. The result leaves audiences spellbound.

Happiest when they're dancing, Bobby and Elaine love performing for a live audience.

49

JOE FEENEY

Joe Feeney's rich Irish tenor voice has thrilled audiences for decades—particularly the ladies, who he's *always* been able to charm!

Joe & Myron

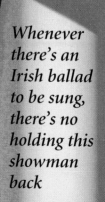

Whenever there's an Irish ballad to be sung, there's no holding this showman back

GUY HOVIS

Guy Hovis joined the Lawrence Welk Television Show in 1970. He sings everything from Country and Gospel to Love Songs—melting many hearts in the process! He is also a very talented guitarist.

"The Wichita Lineman"

GAIL & RON

These versatile and energetic performers are best known for their smooth, rich-blending vocal harmonies.

Gail, Sandi & Mary Lou

Ron, Gail & Michael

ARTHUR DUNCAN

Arthur is always a big hit with audiences. He was born to dance, and quite simply, loves every minute of it.

Arthur keeps the art of tap dancing alive

His warm, engaging personality comes through in every step

ANACANI

First discovered by Lawrence at the Welk Resort Center in San Diego, Anacani's Spanish songs and Latin beauty have won her a large and dedicated following since she first appeared on the show in 1973.

HENRY CUESTA

One of the finest musicians of our time, Henry Cuesta is a clarinetist extraordinaire. Listening to Henry play is an experience audiences treasure.

Henry's many performances of Lawrence's favorite Dixieland pieces kept toes a tappin'.

TOM NETHERTON

Tom's rich voice and "towering" presence make him a prominent member of the Welk Musical Family. A deep faith resonates from the religious songs and ballads he performs so very powerfully.

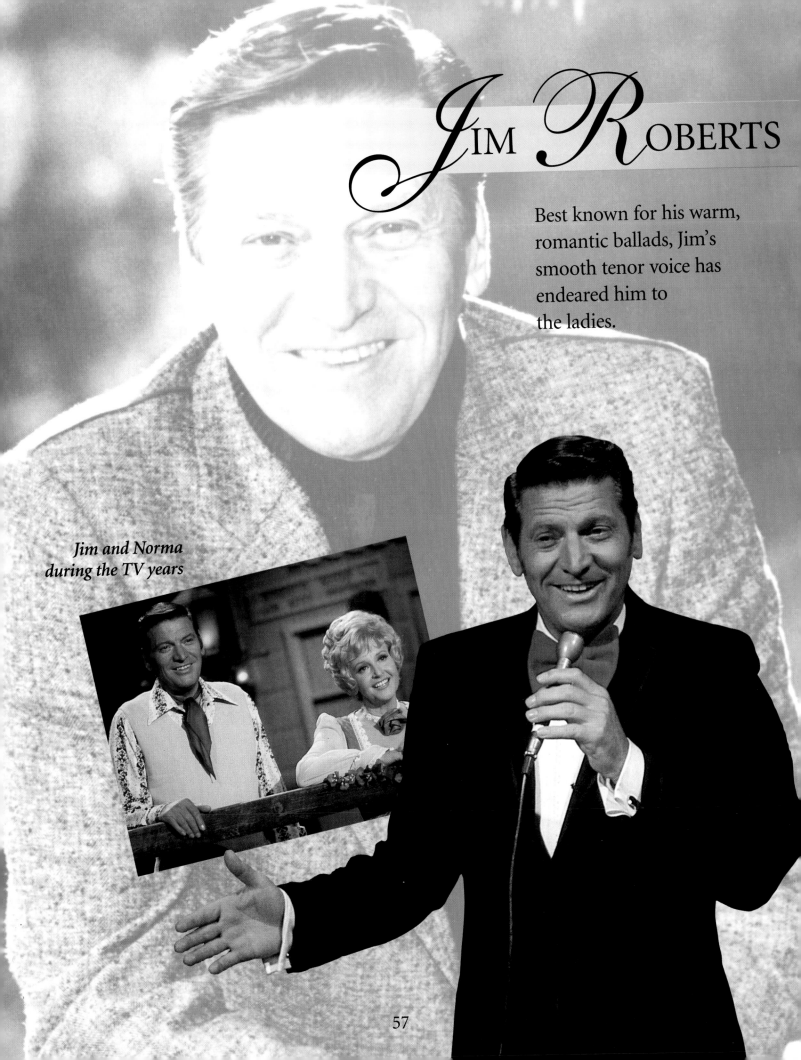

JIM ROBERTS

Best known for his warm, romantic ballads, Jim's smooth tenor voice has endeared him to the ladies.

Jim and Norma during the TV years

JACK IMEL

From a happy-go-lucky dancer and marimba player to showman and assistant producer of the Lawrence Welk Television Show, Jack Imel continues to enrich the Welk Show in Branson.

Jack enjoys a quick tap dance routine with Mary Lou

PETE FOUNTAIN

Pete performed on the T.V. Show in the late '50s. He is one of the all-time jazz greats and continues to play Lawrence's personal favorite— Dixieland.

New Orleans is still home to Pete where he plays in his own nightclub

59

AVA BARBER

It's a delight to listen to the rich, warm tone of Ava's pure and natural country-western voice.

A native Southerner, she's truly "a country gal"

DICK DALE

An all-around entertainer, Dick plays the saxophone, sings, acts and dances. His warm, outgoing presence is felt on, as well as, off stage.

Dick Dale joined the Lawrence Welk Television Show in 1951

Larry Welk, Lawrence's son, is CEO and chairman of the Welk family of companies. He was instrumental in bringing his father's show to Branson. His wife Lynn supervised the decoration of the Branson Resort and was also responsible for the Ozark Mountain Christmas decorations for which the company has won numerous awards. Lynn's sister, Kim Hill, handmade all the window coverings for the resort.

Dear Friends:

It has been more than 70 years since my dad left the farm with his accordion and a dream of being able to bring music and happiness into the lives of others. He loved his life and was thrilled to be able to bring his TV show into millions of homes each week. But, nothing brought him more personal happiness than being able to entertain in front of a live audience. Wouldn't he have loved Branson!

We, the members of his family, are very proud of the legacy, and privileged and dedicated to keeping his dream and music alive.

Fondly,

Larry Welk

Welk Family photograph taken at the Grand Opening of the Welk Resort Center, May 6, 1994 (relationship to Lawrence noted beneath)

(front row, L to R): Tracey Welk (Larry Welk III's wife), Robert[1] & Shirley[2] Fredricks (daughter & her husband), Katie Segall (great-granddaughter), Fern Welk (wife), Donna Mack (daughter), Larry & Lynn Welk (son & his wife), Lindy Welk† (Kevin Welk's wife).

(back row, L to R): Larry Welk III (grandson), Laura‡‡ & Jeff Segall (granddaughter & her husband), David Fredricks (grandson), Jon & Tracy Fredricks (grandson & his wife), Lisa & Paul Parker (granddaughter & her husband), Robert Fredricks, Jr. (grandson), Jenny & Jim Mack (grandson & his wife), Ryan Mack (great-grandson), Christine Mack (granddaughter), Kevin Welk (grandson), David Mack[1]† (grandson).*

Indicates employment at a Welk family company:
  [1] *Member of the Board of Directors*   [2] *Executive Director of The Lawrence Welk Foundation*
  †Welk Direct Marketing   *‡‡ The Welk Resort Center, Escondido*
  * The Welk Music Group

Jon Fredricks, Lawrence's grandson, is Vice President and General Manager of the Welk Resort Center and Champagne Theatre. His wife Tracy, the first Marketing Director at the new resort, has returned as Financial Controller after taking time off to have their first child.

Keep a

in your